STORY-WRITING SANDWICH PROMPTS

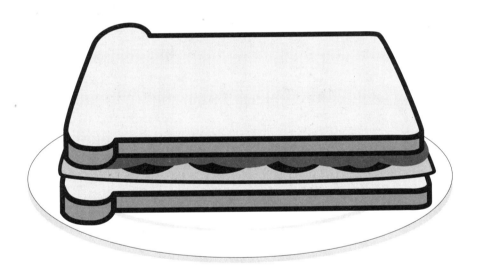

Teresa Klepinger

New York • Toronto • London • Auckland • Sydney
Mexico City • New Delhi • Hong Kong • Buenos Aires

DEDICATION

For Dave, Sara, and Lauren,
who always believe in me.

And for all the wonderful children,
who amaze me with their unlimited imaginations.

Cover design: Tannaz Fassihi
Interior design: Michelle H. Kim
Interior Illustrator: Marybeth Rivera

Images ©: 56–59 top left: Aluna1/iStockphoto; top center: Ben Davis/The Noun Project; top right: Arthur Shlain/The Noun Project; center left: Alex Muravev/The Noun Project; center: Mario Bieh/The Noun Project; center right: Tatiana Kravchenko/iStockphoto; bottom left: Alex Vaughn/The Noun Project; bottom center: artworkbean/The Noun Project; bottom right: uraj Sedlák/The Noun Project.

ISBN: 978-1-338-22715-4

Table of Contents

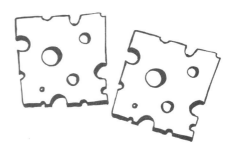

BOTTOM SLICE PROMPTS — 33

THE BREAD PROMPTS — 44

APPENDIX — 55

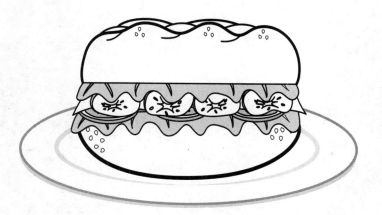

Dear Teachers,

What turns bread paired with turkey or peanut butter or cheese into a sandwich? The answer is *structure*—a top slice of bread, then the filling, and a bottom slice of bread. What turns some sentences into a story? Same thing: giving them a structure—a beginning, a middle, and an end.

Welcome to **Story-Writing Sandwich Prompts**! The 40 skill-building reproducibles in this book will help your students see that every story has a structure, just like a sandwich. It will also help give them the tools they need to become agile, inspired writers.

The prompts are grouped into the elements of a sandwich:

Top Slices
(Writing the Middle and End)

Fillings
(Writing the Beginning and End)

Bottom Slices
(Writing the Beginning and Middle)

The Bread
(Writing Just the Middle)

These exciting prompts offer students practice introducing characters, establishing settings, developing plots, writing dialogue, crafting satisfying conclusions, and more. (For a list of state standards, see box on page 10.) In addition, they're a great way to boost writing confidence—even among your most reluctant scribes. With sandwich prompts, everyone succeeds!

These open-ended prompts can be used in so many ways. Pass them out in the morning to get those creative juices flowing. Use them at the end of the day as a rewarding cool-down activity. Offer them to students who love creative writing as well as those who struggle to generate story ideas. Put them in a learning center for kids to enjoy individually, in pairs, or in groups. You can even send them home for playful, skill-building homework assignments.

Share **Story-Writing Sandwich Prompts** with your class today, and watch all your students write happily ever after.

Warmly,

Teresa Klepinger

GETTING STARTED WITH THE PROMPTS

Sandwich prompts are so easy to use! A quick, fifteen-minute model lesson is all your students will need to use the reproducible pages independently. You might also share one or all of the Planning Pages, which provide pre-writing support related to developing characters, settings, plots, details, and more. (See pages 56–59 in the Appendix.) Here are some quick how-tos for getting started with each of the four types of prompts.

Completing "Top Slice" Prompts
Writing the Middle and End

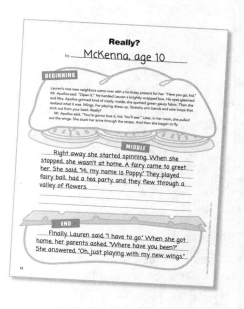

These prompts present the beginnings of stories and contain the elements a writer must provide to kick off a good tale. They identify a main character, a setting, and the "Something happens!" moment. What your students will provide next are the "filling" and the "bottom slice."

Choose a prompt, read it together, and ask:

1. What is the "Something happens!" moment that gives the main character a problem or sets the main character off on an adventure?

2. How will the main character try to solve the problem, or what events will take place in your tale?

3. What will be the moment the problem is solved or the adventure ends?

4. How will the main character be changed at the end of the story?

In writing the filling, your writers can let their imaginations run wild. You'll be surprised at the creative ways their characters will try to get out of scrapes or go off on exploits. Help your students keep the saga on track by making sure it sticks with the main character and the main "Something happens!" situation.

TIP Guide students to identify the point of view in the story—first person, second person, third person, etc.—and remind them to keep it consistent.

Bring the group back together after they've had time to write the middle of their stories. It is now time for their character to solve the problem or end the adventure. It is also time to show how the character has changed. *She is a hero! He has solved the mystery!* Allow the students time to write the end of their stories.

TIP Guide students to resolve the final conflict quickly because once readers know how a tale ends interest will wane.

Story-Writing Sandwich Prompts © Teresa Klepinger • Scholastic Inc.

Completing "Filling" Prompts
Writing the Beginning and End

When students get prompts with only the sandwich filling, they'll need to complete the top and the bottom slices of bread—otherwise known as the beginning and end of the story. The middle of a story does provide information about the main character as well as his or her adventure or problem. However, it does not indicate how that main character got into the fix—that is for your writers to decide!

Read the prompt together and identify:

1. Who is the main character?

2. What is the setting? (The prompt may not identify it. Brainstorm some possibilities.)

3. What problem is the main character trying to solve? Or what exciting event is taking place? Again, there may be many possibilities.

4. Brainstorm how the main character got into this situation.

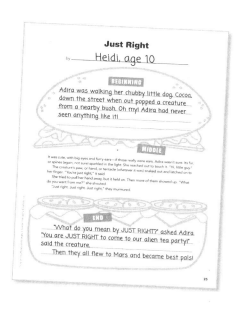

A fun thing to do is to ask the students to close their eyes and visualize the setting. What colors do they see? What sounds do they hear? What scents do they smell? What do the surroundings look like? How do they feel? Discuss students' thoughts and/ or encourage them to jot some quick notes before they begin writing.

Give your students ample time to write the beginning of the story. Then bring them back together and ask: "How does the main character finally solve this problem?" or "What happens next that ends the story?" Remind kids that the conclusion should "make sense" and flow directly from the situation the main character faces in the middle of the tale. Give them time to write the ending, then share their results together or in small groups.

TIP The first time or two that you use these prompts, brainstorming together and sharing ideas is helpful. After that, suggest that students keep their ideas secret. That way you'll get a wider variety of stories. Ideas are like germs—they're contagious! Once someone shares an idea, it gets stuck in everyone else's heads.

INVITE KIDS TO WRITE MORE

Do some of your students want to write longer stories than the reproducibles allow? No worries. Invite them to use the reproducible "Story Extender" on page 60 to continue their tales. Kids simply cut and tape the insert in place for an extra-long, extra-delectable story!

Completing "Bottom Slice" Prompts
Writing the Beginning and Middle

These prompts present the ending of the story. They showcase the main character concluding an adventure, or solving a problem (or failing to). There may be many possible ways the main character got into this situation.

Choose a prompt. Read it together and ask:

1. Where is the main character?

2. What problem did he or she have to solve? Or what adventure did he or she go on?

3. How did the main character get into this situation?

4. What did the main character do to try to solve the problem?

Remind writers that there is never one right answer, and half the fun is coming up with lots of possibilities.

Give the class time to write an opening that introduces the main character, the setting, and the "Something happens!" part of the story. Pause to check in with them and reiterate the elements of a beginning. Then allow time to write the middle, encouraging them to make it exciting!

TIP Sometimes students get carried away with a fun idea and send the story in a direction that is difficult to match to the given ending. Check in with the class and remind them that their story must end with the prompt.

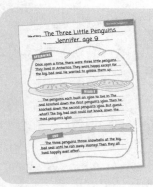

CREATE YOUR OWN SANDWICH PROMPT

Do you or your students want to create original sandwich prompts? Great idea! Just choose a blank template from pages 61–64, fill it with text, and photocopy. Voila! You just created a customized prompt to share with the class.

Completing "The Bread" Prompts

Writing Just the Middle

This prompt presents the beginning of a story, introducing the main character, the setting, and the "Something happens!" moment. It also provides the conclusion of the story, in which children learn how the tale is resolved. What happened in the middle? This is for your students to decide.

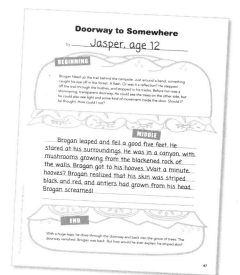

Choose a prompt. Read it together and ask:

1. Who is the main character?

2. What is the setting?

3. What is the "Something happens!" moment?

4. How does the main character change at the end of the story?

5. What brought about this change?

Brainstorm together all the ways the main character could have tried to solve the problem, or all the stops along the way of the adventure, before the story's conclusion. Allow time to write, then share!

TIP Guide students to look for clues that inform readers about the character's emotional state. Does he shout? Does she giggle? Is a facial expression mentioned? What do these things tell us about the character?

TIP If kids get stuck or experience writer's block, simply ask them to tell you what they think will happen next.

10 SUPER IDEAS FOR USING SANDWICH PROMPTS

1. Brainstorm vocabulary words that might go with the prompt. There may be a few (*tendril, blemish, exquisite*). This will help students generate ideas and use rich, specific language in their stories.

2. Challenge your students to switch the point of view of the story—first person to third, third person to second, etc.

3. If students write on tablets or laptops, add a technology lesson by using "Find/Replace" to change the name of the main character.

4. Allow your students to act out their stories.

5. Invite students who like to draw to illustrate their stories.

6. Divide the class into small groups of four to six, and let them complete a prompt together.

7. Collect student stories into a class book where they can read each other's work. Group the stories into chapters with a copy of the prompt at the beginning of each one.

8. Put the book in a writing center where students can choose to use it.

9. Encourage students to create their own prompts for classmates to complete. You may use the templates included in this book (see pages 61–64).

10. Play a "round robin" game where each student adds just one sentence to the tale.

Meeting the Standards

The lessons in this book support the College and Career Readiness Anchor Standards for Reading in Grades K–12. These broad standards, which serve as the basis for many state standards, were developed to establish rigorous educational expectations with the goal of providing students nationwide with a quality education that prepares them for college and careers.

GRADE 3

- Write narratives to develop real or imagined experiences or events using effective technique, descriptive details, and clear event sequences.
- Establish a situation and introduce a narrator and/or characters; organize an event sequence that unfolds naturally.
- Use dialogue and descriptions of actions, thoughts, and feelings to develop experiences and events or show the response of characters to situations.
- Use temporal words and phrases to signal event order.
- Provide a sense of closure.

GRADE 4

- Write narratives to develop real or imagined experiences or events using effective technique, descriptive details, and clear event sequences.
- Orient the reader by establishing a situation and introducing a narrator and/or characters; organize an event sequence that unfolds naturally.
- Use dialogue and description to develop experiences and events or show the responses of characters to situations.
- Use a variety of transitional words and phrases to manage the sequence of events.
- Use concrete words and phrases and sensory details to convey experiences and events precisely.
- Provide a conclusion that follows from the narrated experiences or events.

GRADE 5

- Write narratives to develop real or imagined experiences or events using effective technique, descriptive details, and clear event sequences.
- Orient the reader by establishing a situation and introducing a narrator and/or characters; organize an event sequence that unfolds naturally.
- Use narrative techniques, such as dialogue, description, and pacing, to develop experiences and events or show the responses of characters to situations.
- Use a variety of transitional words, phrases, and clauses to manage the sequence of events.
- Use concrete words and phrases and sensory details to convey experiences and events precisely.
- Provide a conclusion that follows from the narrated experiences or events.

GRADE 6

- Write narratives to develop real or imagined experiences or events using effective technique, relevant descriptive details, and well-structured event sequences.
- Engage and orient the reader by establishing a context and introducing a narrator and/or characters; organize an event sequence that unfolds naturally and logically.
- Use narrative techniques, such as dialogue, pacing, and description, to develop experiences, events, and/or characters.
- Use a variety of transition words, phrases, and clauses to convey sequence and signal shifts from one time frame or setting to another.
- Use precise words and phrases, relevant descriptive details, and sensory language to convey experiences and events.
- Provide a conclusion that follows from the narrated experiences or events.

Source: © Copyright 2010 National Governors Association Center for Best Practices and Council of Chief State School Officers. All rights reserved.

TOP SLICE PROMPTS

Writing the Middle and End

Really?

by _____

Lauren's nice new neighbors came over with a birthday present for her. "Here you go, kid," Mr. Apollos said. "Open it." He handed Lauren a brightly wrapped box. His eyes gleamed and Mrs. Apollos grinned kind of crazily. Inside, she spotted green gauzy fabric. Then she realized what it was. Wings. For playing dress-up. Stretchy arm bands and wire loops that stick out from your back. Really?

Mr. Apollos said, "You're gonna love it, kid. You'll see." Later, in her room, she pulled out the wings. She stuck her arms through the straps. And then she began to fly.

MIDDLE

_____

_____

_____

_____

_____

_____

END

_____

_____

_____

Story-Writing Sandwich Prompts © Teresa Klepinger • Scholastic Inc.

Dinner Is Served

by _____

BEGINNING

Alma's Dad coughed and sneezed and groaned. "I'm sorry, honey," he said. "I just can't get myself out of bed to cook dinner."

"That's okay," Alma said. "Leave it to me. I've been watching the cooking channel. Go back to sleep, and when you wake up a scrumptious dinner will be waiting." Her dad grunted like he didn't believe her. In the kitchen, Alma gathered a little of this and some of that from the refrigerator, the pantry, and the shelves. Then she set to work.

MIDDLE

_____

_____

_____

_____

_____

_____

END

_____

_____

_____

Dog Walking

by _____

Whitley's dog-walking business was getting busy. At the Williams' house, she found the leash and slipped into Harley's pen to clip it on. The big dog jumped and slobbered and whacked her legs with his tail.

On their way out, Whitley yelled at the massive dog, "Harley! Slow down!" He just pulled harder. Whitley grabbed the loop end with both hands. "Harley, heel!" *Does he even know that word?* "No! Stay! Sit! Bad dog!" His ears didn't even turn back. He was intent on following his nose. Then a cat darted in front of them.

MIDDLE

_____

_____

_____

_____

_____

_____

_____

END

_____

_____

_____

Instant Success

by _____

Juan and Aisha hit "Enter" and watched their website go live. "I wonder how long till someone orders one." Juan whispered. They stared at the screen, holding their breath. Nothing happened.

Hunger tore them away, and after a quick lunch they returned to find not one order, not ten, but 945. "Wahoo! We're rich!" Juan jumped in the air and swung Aisha around in circles. Then they stopped. Their smiles disappeared.

Aisha took a deep breath. "How in the world are we going to make nine hundred and forty five of these?"

MIDDLE

_____
_____
_____
_____
_____
_____
_____

END

_____
_____
_____

Night Builders

by _____

McKinley yawned and crawled into bed, leaving her Lego creation on the floor. In the morning, she was shocked to see that her half-built Lego monster was finished, complete with spikes and fangs. *Did I sleepwalk? Or, I guess, sleepbuild?* That night she left the monster and an almost finished volcano next to her bed. The next morning the volcano was complete, and an entire Lego monster world stretched across the floor, her windowsill, and the top of her dresser.

I've got to find out who's doing this!

MIDDLE

_____
_____
_____
_____
_____
_____
_____

END

_____
_____
_____

Story-Writing Sandwich Prompts © Teresa Klepinger • Scholastic Inc.

Protesters Unite!

by _____

BEGINNING

The supermarket fruits and vegetables were tired of being rejected for tiny blemishes. They were tired of squeezes and sharp fingernails. One night, the giant baker potato called a meeting. "Fruits! Vegetables! It's time to protest!" The produce perked up. "Are we sick of this treatment?"

There came a resounding "YES!"

"Here's what we must do," the potato continued. "We'll write a message to the humans. Carrots, celery, and zucchini, you're the straight lines. Apples, tomatoes, and onions, you're the dots. Bananas, you're the curves. This is what we'll say." The letters quickly took shape.

MIDDLE

_____

_____

_____

_____

_____

_____

END

_____

_____

_____

Supersize Me

by _____

Ahmed escaped the summer heat into the cool of the frozen yogurt store. He grabbed a container and twisted the handle for his favorite flavor. When the cup was full, Ahmed twisted the handle to *off*. But the yogurt didn't stop flowing. He pushed harder. It still didn't stop. The yogurt spilled over the sides and onto his shoes and the floor.

"Help! Something's wrong!" he yelled. "It won't stop!"

The cashier skidded up to him shouting, "What did you do?" He grabbed the handle and pushed it back and forth. The yogurt kept on coming. And now it gushed even faster.

MIDDLE

_____

_____

_____

_____

_____

_____

_____

_____

END

_____

_____

_____

_____

The Secret of Dogs

by _____

BEGINNING

Lexie squeezed under the fence and into her backyard just before her boy got home from school. When he greeted her, she barked and wagged her tail properly. This time, though, she had important business. After months of discussion, the Dog Council had made a decision. Today was the day.

Lexie faced her boy. She looked intently into his eyes and held perfectly still. The boy cocked his head. "What is it, girl? Why are you looking at me like that?"

Lexie sat and cleared her throat. "The time has come," she said. "You must know the Secret of Dogs."

MIDDLE

_____

_____

_____

_____

_____

_____

_____

END

_____

_____

_____

_____

Wild Things

by _____

BEGINNING

Sophia lay on her bed and flipped open her new book of stories: "Island Escapade," "Cave Mystery," "Wild Things in the Wilderness." She picked "Wild Things," since it reminded her of her favorite book from when she was little.

Quite soon, she was lost in the story, trekking through the forest, desperate for water, listening to wolves drawing closer. She began to sweat. Hawks cried and leaves crunched underfoot. She tore her eyes from the page and gasped. The book had become real! Vines hung from the ceiling, and the walls had become the world all around.

MIDDLE

_____
_____
_____
_____
_____
_____
_____

END

_____
_____
_____

Queen Cinderella

by _____

Queen Cinderella and King Charming returned from their honeymoon and settled in to life at the castle. Everything was beautiful. Everything was peaceful. Everything was . . . boring. Cinderella decided she needed a job to do. She looked around the kingdom, talked to the people, and made up her mind. "Charming, dear," she said one day. "I'm starting a business." Then she told him her idea.

_____

_____

_____

_____

_____

_____

_____

_____

_____

_____

FILLING PROMPTS

Writing the Beginning and End

Closer and Closer

by _____

BEGINNING

_____

_____

_____

_____

_____

MIDDLE

Minjun crouched in the bushes. Did it see him? He held his breath, keeping as still as possible. He could hear it getting closer and closer. *Thump-scrape. Thump-scrape.* Should he run? His folded legs were getting uncomfortable. His leg was cramping. But moving would make noise. *Thump-scrape. Thump-scrape.*

He couldn't stand it. He had to stretch his cramping leg. Minjun lost his balance. He tumbled forward out into the open, directly in its path. *Thump-scrape.* He scooted backwards, crab-walking at double speed. It saw him.

END

_____

_____

_____

_____

Most Embarrassing Moment

by _____

BEGINNING

_____
_____
_____
_____
_____

MIDDLE

My cheeks reddened and my heart started thumping. Everyone turned and stared. There was no hole to crawl into, nothing to hide behind. I even considered crawling under a table, but I knew I was too old for that. I could act like it was all part of a plan. *Yeah, right.* Or pretend it wasn't me. *Who did that?* Or just run. So that's what I did. All the way home.

I didn't really escape, though. The phone rang that night.

Mom answered it. "She did WHAT?"

END

_____
_____
_____
_____

Just Right

by _____

BEGINNING

MIDDLE

It was cute, with big eyes and furry ears—if those really were ears. Adira wasn't sure. Its fur, or spines (again, not sure) sparkled in the light. She reached out to touch it. "Hi, little guy."

The creature's paw, or hand, or tentacle (whatever it was) snaked out and latched on to her finger. "You're just right," it said.

She tried to pull her hand away, but it held on. Then more of them showed up. "What do you want from me?" she shouted.

"Just right. Just right. Just right," they murmured.

END

Lost and Found

by _____

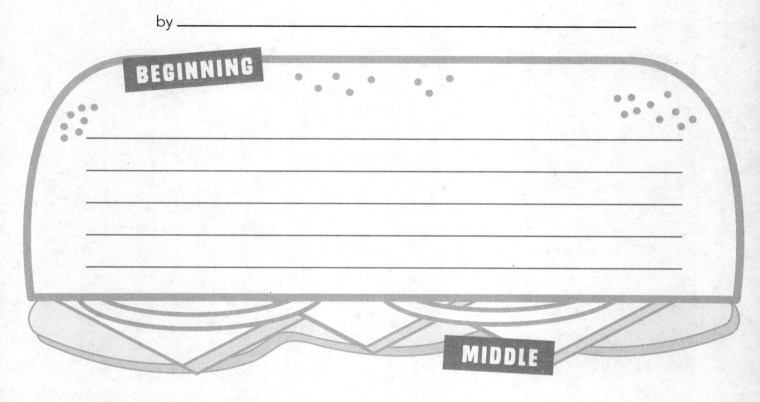

BEGINNING

MIDDLE

Slowly the kitten came out, sniffing, darting its eyes in every direction. Anna held her hand motionless until the kitten rubbed its head against her knuckles. She slid her palm under its belly and lifted.

"Oh! You're a feather!" she said. Every rib jutted from its sides. Stroking its back, the knobby spine bumped along her hand. Its coat lay dull and rough. She tucked the scrawny creature into her jacket. "You poor thing. You're coming home with me, no matter what Mom says."

END

Press Conference

by _____

BEGINNING

_____
_____
_____
_____
_____

MIDDLE

The reporters spotted me and started to run in my direction. They shouted questions and shoved their microphones in my face. I was going to have to talk about it. When I raised my hands, the crowd hushed.

"I know you all want to hear from me," I said. "So I'll explain it, but just this once."

Halfway through, they began shouting again. "How did you feel when you heard the news?" "What are you going to do next?" "How do you think your life will change?"

I couldn't even answer one question before three more came at me.

I gave up.

END

_____
_____
_____

Race to the Top

by _____

BEGINNING

_____
_____
_____
_____
_____

MIDDLE

Mina grabbed the branch above her head and lifted both feet onto the thickest vine that snaked up the trunk of the outlandish tree. Could she climb faster than it was growing? If she couldn't, she'd never reach her brother at the top, and the plant might carry him away.

She braced her foot on the next fat branch and pushed herself up. A vine twined itself around her wrist. She shook it off. Then another wound around her ankle. She kicked free. She must climb faster.

END

_____
_____
_____
_____
_____

Rescue

by _____

BEGINNING

_____

_____

_____

_____

MIDDLE

"How are we going to get down?" Carson cried.

Maddie grabbed him by the shoulders. "Carson! Calm down! Just do what I tell you." She pulled off her scarf. "Give me your belt."

Her brother quickly handed it over. "I get it," he said. "That will work. Maybe use my shirt and socks, too."

Maddie tied them all together and tugged. The knots held. "Okay," she said. "This is what we're going to do."

END

_____

_____

_____

_____

The Signal

by _____

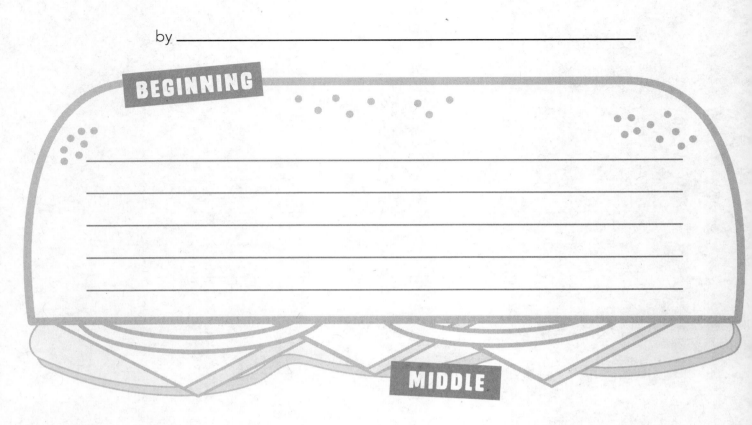

BEGINNING

MIDDLE

"Don't do *anything* until you get the signal. Got it?" he said.

"Yes, sir," Kyle answered. That night, Kyle waited until he was positive everyone else was asleep, then silently slid out of bed and tiptoed to the window. His breath fogged the glass, and he wiped it with his sleeve. He stared into the darkness. Waiting. Watching.

A flash. *Was that it?* He peered intently, holding his breath. *Yes! There it is.* Three long flashes, then two short flashes. Three long. Two short. *The signal.* He began to get ready.

END

Watch This!

by _____

BEGINNING

_____
_____
_____
_____

MIDDLE

"It's true," Collin said. "Watch this." He stared at the lamp on my bedside table, hard. He concentrated so hard his cheeks started to twitch. His skin started to glisten with sweat. Then the lamp started to quiver. It shifted, scooting across the table just a little bit. Collin's mouth compressed into a straight line. Then the lamp started to rise. Just a little bit, maybe an inch.

"Oh man," I said. "That's crazy. Are you doing that?" Collin just stared at the lamp, his whole body tense.

"Collin," I said. "What else can you do?"

END

_____
_____
_____
_____

What's Going On Here?

by _____

BEGINNING

BEGINNING

_____

_____

_____

_____

_____

MIDDLE

The door opened and the principal walked in. Her eyebrows shot to the top of her forehead. Her voice boomed. "What's going on here?"

Everyone froze. Addison squeaked, "It's not what it looks like."

Mrs. Alvarez shut the door behind her. She waited.

Addison blushed and looked around. A few kids shook their heads. A few shrugged their shoulders. She began to explain, and as Mrs. Alvarez listened, her face softened and a smile replaced her tight lips. Finally, when Addison was done, she said, "How can I help?"

END

_____

_____

_____

_____

BOTTOM SLICE PROMPTS

Writing the Beginning and Middle

That Tuesday in June

by _____

BEGINNING

_____

_____

_____

_____

MIDDLE

_____

_____

_____

_____

_____

_____

_____

END

"That was really fun," Zelda the cow said. "Let's do it again sometime."

"Oh, Zelda," Bessie replied. "The poor farmer might have a heart attack. You saw his face. I thought he'd fall over from the shock."

So the cows acted like cows from then on, and farmer Johnson never told a soul about that very strange Tuesday in June.

Afternoon at the Zoo

by _____

BEGINNING

_____
_____
_____
_____

MIDDLE

_____
_____
_____
_____
_____

END

Hudson slammed the gate shut on the last zebra. I thought this was supposed to be a nice afternoon at the zoo, he thought. Sheesh! He walked back to the tree along the path and looked up into the branches. "You can come down now, Mom."

"Are you sure? What about the ostriches?" a hidden voice answered.

A zookeeper stepped up beside Hudson. "They're all back in their pens, ma'am. And we apologize for the faulty locks." He reached an arm up to the tree. "This will never happen again," he said. "We promise."

Broken Leg Woes

by _____

_____
_____
_____
_____

MIDDLE

_____
_____
_____
_____
_____
_____

END

Three days later, Tate rolled his wheelchair down toward the classroom, his leg sticking straight out in front of him. The kids would freak, just like last Friday when the paramedics pulled up to the school.

He could hear excited voices coming from behind the door. He knocked. The room went silent. Then Hakima threw the door open. "Surprise!" Kids wore party hats, tossed balloons, and passed out cake.

For the next half hour, Tate answered questions about ambulances, x-rays, wheelchairs and whether he'd ever try THAT again. Okay, he thought. This won't be so bad after all.

Story-Writing Sandwich Prompts © Teresa Klepinger • Scholastic Inc.

Farewell

by _____

BEGINNING

_____
_____
_____
_____

MIDDLE

_____
_____
_____
_____
_____
_____

END

The dragon dropped lightly to the ground and Sara slid off. "My wing appears to be healed at last," he said. "Thank you for providing a place for me to heal."

"Will I ever see you again?" Sara asked.

"You have many years ahead of you," the dragon rumbled. "Who knows what the future holds?" Then he leaped from the ground, spread his enormous wings, and pumped himself into the air. Sara watched him climb higher and higher. Then, confined to the earth once more, she followed the trail down the hillside to home.

Hands-On Learning

by _____

BEGINNING

_____

_____

_____

_____

MIDDLE

_____

_____

_____

_____

_____

_____

END

In an instant, the jungle disappeared and the classroom became normal again. No more vines and monkeys and creepy-crawlies. The air cooled. Mr. McSweeney tucked his wand back in his pocket. "And that concludes our unit on the rainforest," he said. He smiled and patted that pocket again. "On Monday, we'll start learning about Antarctica."

Story Writing Sandwich Prompts © Tonya Kinzinger, Scholastic Inc.

Riding the Rails

by _____

BEGINNING

_____
_____
_____
_____

MIDDLE

_____
_____
_____
_____
_____
_____

END

Hours later, the station came into view, and the great steam engine slowed. The conductor turned to me and said, "You gotta get off here, kid. You'll have to wait till your pa comes for you, and horses are a might slower than trains." He put his hand on my shoulder. "And kid, don't try that again." Then he winked.

He knew, just like I did. My future lay on those tracks, and nothing would keep me away.

Stranded

by _____

BEGINNING

_____
_____
_____
_____

MIDDLE

_____
_____
_____
_____
_____

END

The sound I'd waited so long for reached my ears. An airplane! I raced to the beach, guarding my little flame with my hand. With a touch of the torch to the dry grass, the signal fire quickly grew. I checked the SOS spelled out with branches. Still in place. The plane headed my way. Black smoke from my burning tire belched into the air. I waved my arms, jumping, screaming, "Here I am! I'm here! See me!"

The plane dipped lower, then flew straight toward me. It dipped its wings left, right, left, right. Finally, I was saved.

The Finish Line

by _____

BEGINNING

_____

_____

_____

_____

MIDDLE

_____

_____

_____

_____

_____

_____

END

The finish line finally came into sight. With the last of my energy, I pushed my legs as fast as they could possibly go, but there wasn't much left in me. As soon as I crossed the finish line I collapsed to the ground.

A roaring noise filled my ears. No, it was voices, cheering, clapping. For who? I had come in dead last. I opened my eyes and saw everyone gathering around me, lifting me, carrying me on their shoulders.

They knew. They appreciated what I had done back there. They cared. It was worth it.

The Haircut

by _____

BEGINNING

_____
_____
_____
_____

MIDDLE

_____
_____
_____
_____
_____
_____
_____

END

A sense of doom came over Maria. She realized she had no choice. There was only one solution. With trembling fingers, she picked up the scissors in one hand, grabbed her hair in the other, and started cutting. In about a minute, her long, thick, wavy, glossy hair lay in strands on the floor. She quickly scooped it up and hid it. No time for tears, she thought. She changed into the new clothes, opened the door, and stepped into her new life.

Story-Writing Sandwich Prompts © Teresa Klepinger • Scholastic Inc.

Under the Sea

by _____

BEGINNING

_____

_____

_____

_____

MIDDLE

_____

_____

_____

_____

_____

_____

_____

END

With a final flip of her tail, the mermaid launched off the high rock and down, down, into the water.

"NOOOOOO!" the two voices cried out from above.

She surfaced briefly, looking back at them. Then, with a small smile, she ducked below the waves, never to be seen again.

THE BREAD PROMPTS

Writing Just the Middle

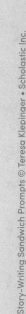Story-Writing Sandwich Prompts © Teresa Klepinger • Scholastic Inc.

Beach Find

by _____

BEGINNING

Sam jogged down to the beach. Early mornings were the best. He'd get first pick of whatever the tide washed up. Suddenly, his big toe caught on something, and he landed face first in the sand. *What was that?* It wasn't a rock, and it wasn't a piece of driftwood. He began to dig around the object.

MIDDLE

_____

_____

_____

_____

_____

_____

_____

_____

END

After burying it in the new hiding place, Sam slowly walked home. His life would never be the same, he knew. But what a life it was going to be!

Birthday Dinner

by _____

Fisher sat down to his birthday dinner. "Honey," his mom said. "This is a very important birthday. For many generations, everyone in our family has had a very special dinner on this day." She set a plate in front of him. In the center rested a cube of . . . maybe Jello?

"Go ahead, son," his dad said. His eyes shone expectantly. "Take a bite. Just like I did on my birthday."

MIDDLE

_____
_____
_____
_____
_____
_____
_____

END

Fisher stayed home from school for a few days to get used to it. Soon, though, he could say, believe it or not, that he had the coolest family in the world.

Story-Writing Sandwich Prompts © Teresa Klepinger • Scholastic Inc.

Doorway to Somewhere

by _____

BEGINNING

Brogan hiked up the trail behind the campsite. Just around a bend, something caught his eye off in the forest. A flash. Or was it a reflection? He stepped off the trail through the bushes, and stopped in his tracks. Before him was a shimmering, transparent doorway. He could see the trees on the other side, but he could also see light and some kind of movement inside the door. Should I? he thought. How could I not?

MIDDLE

_____
_____
_____
_____
_____
_____
_____
_____

END

With a huge leap, he dove through the doorway and back into the grove of trees. The doorway vanished. Brogan was back. But how would he ever explain his striped skin?

Hundred Dollar Bill

by _____

BEGINNING

Keisha opened her pencil box. Out fell a one-hundred dollar bill and a folded piece of paper. "Use it well, and you'll get another," it said.

At first she wanted to spend it on herself. But would she get another one? Then she had a better idea.

MIDDLE

_____

_____

_____

_____

_____

_____

_____

_____

_____

END

Keisha stood before the cheering audience. She looked around at the sea of faces and smiled. The audience applauded as she stepped to the microphone. "Thank you," she said. "And thank you to my mystery friend who started it all."

Make a Wish

by _____

BEGINNING

Aiden cranked the handle on the little music box. The lid snapped open and up popped a tiny clown. The little figure held a sign, and Aiden bent close to read it. "One wish I grant, but beware. With that wish you must take care."

MIDDLE

_____
_____
_____
_____
_____
_____
_____
_____

END

How was I supposed to know THAT would happen, Aiden thought. "Take care" is right! He managed to put things right before anyone found out, though, and he told no one the story for many years.

Metamorphosis

by _____

Manuel leaned on the stall door and watched his brand-new horse munching hay. He couldn't take his eyes off Sparkle as she chewed, swished her tail, and snorted. But why did she keep turning her head to rub her muzzle against her side, like she had an itch? First one side, then the other.

But then Manuel began to see why. Two matching lumps were forming under her skin. They grew and stretched until each one split a tiny bit and Manuel could see . . . feathers. His horse was growing wings.

MIDDLE

_____

_____

_____

_____

_____

_____

_____

_____

END

Sparkle folded her wings and nuzzled Manuel. "That was amazing, Sparkle," he whispered. He wanted to go up again and again, but would he get to? Now he knew no fence would hold her. She was his only if she chose to be. Sparkle turned and walked into her stall.

Surprise Party

by _____

"Brooklyn is coming to my party?" Courtney fought to control her voice. "Mom, she's the new girl. We don't know anything about her!"

"All the more reason to invite her," her mother replied. "Maybe she'll surprise you."

On the day of the party Courtney's friends arrived, and the room came alive with laughter and music. Then the doorbell rang one more time. It was Brooklyn.

MIDDLE

_____

_____

_____

_____

_____

_____

_____

END

When she had said goodbye to the last guest, Courtney closed her eyes and leaned her forehead against the door. They got to know Brooklyn all right. And nobody would ever forget a surprise like that.

The Masks

by _____

BEGINNING

Something was going on with Grandpa since he got back from his trip. Joshua knew the answer lay in the closet Grandpa had recently locked up, and now he had finally found the key. He slowly pushed the door open, flipped the light switch, and nearly jumped out of his skin. Masks stared from the walls. Santa Claus and a super hero. An alien, a snake, a fly, even the President. He lifted one down and slipped it on his face.

MIDDLE

_____
_____
_____
_____
_____
_____
_____
_____
_____

END

Now he understood. With a grin, Joshua hung the mask back on the wall and returned the key to its hiding place. *I think I'll be visiting Grandpa a lot more now.*

The Suitcase

by _____

Scott filled the last square inch of his suitcase and just barely managed to get it closed. He was ready to go. His heart beat a little faster at the thought. Is this really happening? With a deep breath, he dragged the suitcase out the door.

MIDDLE

_____

_____

_____

_____

_____

_____

_____

_____

_____

END

At last, the suitcase was completely empty. The faces of the people around him beamed with happiness. The children laughed and ran. One woman gave him a huge hug. No doubt in his mind, it was totally worth it.

The Visitor

by _____

BEGINNING

Lucy tiptoed down the dark hall. Who in the world was cooking in the kitchen with the lights off? She stopped and peeked very carefully around the corner. Moonlight from the window revealed a pot on the stove. A spoon stirred inside it, but no hand guided the spoon. An egg lifted itself out of the carton, cracked against a skillet, and spilled inside. Then the refrigerator door opened, and the light illuminated what she could only describe as a ghost.

MIDDLE

_____

_____

_____

_____

_____

_____

_____

_____

END

"I can stay if no one knows about me," the ghost said. "Except you."

"Really? I promise I won't tell!" Lucy said. She crossed her heart. "One thing, though, cooking in the middle of the night probably isn't the best way to stay a secret."

"I suppose not," he said.

Lucy smiled. "This is going to be so cool."

APPENDIX

Planning Page • Story Extender
Blank Template

Name _____

Top Slice Prompts Planning Page
(Writing the Middle and End)

Title of Story _____

What is the setting of your story?
Who is the main character?
How will your character solve his/her problem?   **(OR: What adventure will the main character go on?)**
How will the story end?

SPICE IT UP!

Check the items you plan on adding to your story to make it extra exciting:

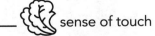

____ sense of sight   ____ sense of touch   ____ sense of smell

____ sense of taste   ____ sense of sound   ____ humor

 ____ emotion   ____ weather   ____ dialogue

Name _____

Filling Prompts Planning Page
(Writing the Beginning and End)

Title of Story _____

What is the setting of your story?
Who is the main character?
What is the "Something happens!" moment?
How will the main character solve the problem or end the adventure?

SPICE IT UP!

Check the items you plan on adding to your story to make it extra exciting:

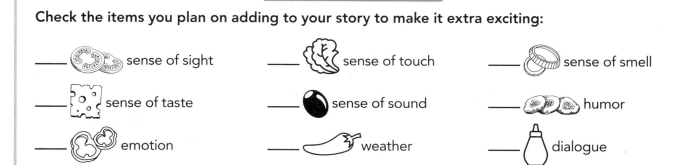

_____ sense of sight   _____ sense of touch   _____ sense of smell

_____ sense of taste   _____ sense of sound   _____ humor

_____ emotion   _____ weather   _____ dialogue

Name _____

Bottom Slice Prompts Planning Page
(Writing the Beginning and Middle)

Title of Story _____

What is the setting of your story?
Who is the main character?
What is the "Something happens!" moment?
How will the main character try to solve the problem or what adventures will he/she have?

SPICE IT UP!

Check the items you plan on adding to your story to make it extra exciting:

 _____ sense of sight   _____ sense of touch   _____ sense of smell

 _____ sense of taste   _____ sense of sound   _____ humor

 _____ emotion   _____ weather   _____ dialogue

Name _____

The Bread Prompts Planning Page
(Writing Just the Middle)

Title of Story _____

What is the setting of your story?
Who is the main character?
What is the "Something happens!" moment?
How will the main character try to solve the problem or what adventures will he/she have?

SPICE IT UP!

Check the items you plan on adding to your story to make it extra exciting:

____ sense of sight   ____ sense of touch   ____ sense of smell

____ sense of taste   ____ sense of sound   ____ humor

 ____ emotion   ____ weather   ____ dialogue

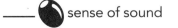

Story Extender Template

_____

_____

_____

_____

_____

_____

_____

_____

_____

_____

_____

_____

_____

_____

_____

_____

_____

_____

_____

Title of Story _____

by _____

BEGINNING

_____

_____

_____

_____

MIDDLE

_____

_____

_____

_____

_____

_____

_____

END

_____

_____

_____

Title of Story _____

by _____

BEGINNING

_____

_____

_____

_____

MIDDLE

_____

_____

_____

_____

_____

END

_____

_____

_____

Title of Story _____

by _____

BEGINNING

_____
_____
_____
_____

MIDDLE

_____
_____
_____
_____
_____
_____

END

_____
_____
_____

Title of Story _____

by _____

BEGINNING

_____
_____
_____
_____

MIDDLE

_____
_____
_____
_____
_____
_____

END

_____
_____
_____